FACEBOOK ADVERTISING:
A FIELD GUIDE FOR AUTO DEALERS

First Edition

Copyright © March 2018
9 Clouds, Inc.
431 N Phillips Ave., Suite 440, Sioux Falls, South Dakota, 57104

Facebook™ is a registered trademark of Facebook, Inc.,
1601 Willow Road Menlo Park CALIFORNIA 94025.

9 Clouds™, the 9 Clouds logo, and the 9C logo are trademarks of 9 Clouds, Inc., 431 N Phillips Ave. Sioux Falls SOUTH DAKOTA 57104. 9 Clouds does not claim ownership of any other trademarks used in this document.

CONTENTS

INTRODUCTION	7
GLOSSARY	14
SETUP	23
TARGETING	42
BUDGETING	44
AD FORMATS	48
RECIPE GUIDE	54
TOP-OF-FUNNEL ADS	57
MIDDLE-OF-FUNNEL ADS	73
BOTTOM-OF-FUNNEL ADS	89
OPTIMIZING	100
CONCLUSION	102

CONTRIBUTORS

SCOTT D. MEYER
INTRODUCTION, SETUP, CONCLUSION

MATT STOFFEL
GLOSSARY, RECIPES

SARAH KLONGERBO
EDITING, RECIPES

JOHN NELSON
DESIGN, RECIPES

RACHEL SPEISER
RECIPES

BETSY SPRENKLE
RECIPES

JADEN MILLER
RECIPES

JACQUELYN JACOBSMA
RECIPES

ALLEN DAY
RECIPES

INTRODUCTION

WELCOME TO FACEBOOK, POPULATION: 2.1 BILLION

Facebook is the modern-day town square. The place where we gather to talk, share, yell, and snoop.

Most importantly for auto and RV dealers, people come to the town square to shop. They might not come with the goal of shopping . . . but just as the sweet aroma of a coffee shop pulls us into a coffee shop, Facebook shows us the products we can't live without — including a new car.

Facebook advertising works for two reasons: attention and data.

FACEBOOK'S ATTENTION

Facebook has our attention. Facebook has more than 2 billion active users, and more than 1.3 billion of those users log in every day. Facebook also owns other popular platforms, such as Instagram, Facebook Messenger, and WhatsApp.

Of all the apps people have on their phones — including Google, YouTube, and Twitter — people spend **20% of all mobile time on Facebook and Instagram**, according to U.S. comScore data.[1] That's more than 50 minutes a day.

The average American spends more than 50 minutes a day on Facebook and Instagram.

Facebook is where you need to be if you want to get your message in front of your intended audience.

FACEBOOK'S DATA

Facebook has a lot of data, stemming from three unique sources: Facebook's user data, integrated third-party databases, and website traffic data.

First, Facebook has all the information we voluntarily provide, such as our name, our age, where we live, what we like, and more.

Second, Facebook purchases third-party data, such as Polk data, financial data, and consumer activity data. This helps Facebook learn what you do offline.

Third, Facebook pixels are voluntarily installed on the majority of websites. These pixels track what a person looks at across the web, even when they are not on Facebook. This information is sent back to Facebook, so it can identify your interests and know exactly when a user starts to shop.

All this data combined gives marketers a wide range of insights to harness when targeting your digital marketing messages. After all, individuals have different interests and are all looking to buy a car at different times.

Instead of plastering your ads everywhere, Facebook advertising allows a marketer to take a surgical approach and hone in on who will be the most interested. By targeting your content to people who will find it relevant to their current needs and wants, you'll find your ideal audience.

> *You can show the right message to the right people at the right time. That's why Facebook is so powerful.*

With Facebook, you have people's attention, and you have the data to know whom to reach. That's why Facebook will continue to aggregate data and dominate advertising.

FACEBOOK, THE SUPER AGGREGATOR

Even more impressive than Facebook's current size is its ability to continue to grow, thanks to its power as a "super aggregator" in the Age of Aggregation.[2]

THE AGE OF AGGREGATION

Business has changed. More specifically, the problem that many businesses solve has changed.

In the past, the big problem was distribution.

A newspaper distributed stories and ideas; a hardware store distributed hammers and nails; a tax consultant distributed tax advice to nearby businesses. It took a lot of investment for someone to build a business that distributed better than these incumbents.

The Internet has changed business by reducing the cost of distribution to zero. It costs basically nothing to share ideas online. It is nearly free to find the perfect hammer and nail and have them sent to your house within days. It is quick to find tax help from people or software — from anywhere in the country or world — whenever your heart desires.

> When distribution costs go to zero, the problem that businesses need to solve is how to match the supply with the demand of potential customers.

When there is endless supply, we don't have the ability to look at all the options. How, then, does a company aggregate all of the potential products/services/information to ensure the right product/service/information is shown to the right person?

FREE SUPPLY, CONTROLLED DEMAND

Facebook is a super aggregator that enjoys free supply and controls demand.

On the supply side, Facebook receives its content for free. All photos, messages, business listings, products in Marketplace, and more are uploaded to Facebook for free by all of its users.

On the demand side, Facebook chooses which of these pieces of content to show to a specific user based on their interests. Facebook learns over time from its data what people like and what they will buy.

In short: Facebook enjoys endless supply and limitless demand, so it acts as the matchmaker in the middle.

When a monopolist enjoys this power, it can quickly decide what else to include in its supply. Facebook is now doing just that, moving from photos and messages to TV, personal communication, and product listings.

THE NETWORK EFFECT

The longer we spend on Facebook, the more it can show us ads and grow its business.

Plus, the more time we spend in Facebook's universe, the more data it collects on our interests, and the better it does at curating the content we most want to see.

What's more, we are all on Facebook because our *friends* are on Facebook. This network effect locks Facebook's dominance in place as it aggregates our relationships, referred to as our "social graph."

Facebook is not only a powerful platform today; it will grow in its dominance.

Following Facebook's outsized role in the 2016 U.S. election, it seems increasingly likely that regulation may come to Facebook, especially for its ads division.

What many are not considering, however, is that regulation will further build a "moat" for Facebook, making it harder for others to compete.

Sure, Facebook doesn't want legislation. Sure, legislation might be good for our privacy. In terms of competition, however, it will be damaging.

If regulation is set up to limit the ability of Facebook to aggregate, it will be even more difficult for other start-ups to follow the same rules.

Legislation may limit some of Facebook's data-gathering tactics — but with a monopoly on our attention and an eye on websites around the world, it will still do a good job of showing the best results to users. Other sites and apps won't have access to the variety of data sources that Facebook has, so they will provide a poorer experience for users, thus encouraging people to stay on Facebook.

Legislation may also limit our ability to share our social graph across networks to ensure greater privacy. Without an ability to move our social graphs, users on social network competitors would have to start from scratch in building their list of friends. Facebook simply has too big of a head start, and legislation furthers this advantage.

Facebook is the best place to advertise. It shows the right ad to the right people at the right time. Thus, this book.

SIGN UP FOR NOTIFICATIONS ON NEW EDITIONS AND ADDITIONAL RESOURCES AT:

9clouds.com/facebook/fieldguide

SUPER HIGHWAY OFF-RAMP

Most marketers use Facebook the same way they use television ads: to blast everyone with the same message. A new mindset is needed to reach the right customers and, most importantly, get them off of Facebook and into your database.

Any dealer could log in and reach potential car buyers based on Facebook's data.

Only your store, however, can run ads to people in your customer relationship management (CRM) system. Facebook should be seen as an off-ramp, a way to get potential buyers into your own database, where you can talk to them and provide a personal experience to help the buyer choose your store.

This field guide walks through what is needed to run professional Facebook ads and lays out general rules that will ensure your ads are more successful.

Then, we provide the most successful recipes we have developed over three years of running more than $2 million worth of ads specifically for auto dealers and RV dealers.

GLOSSARY

As you meander through this book, you might see some terms that make you scratch your head. Digital marketing, and especially Facebook advertising, come with a lot of jargon.

To get you up to speed — or to glance back at when you get lost — here's a glossary to help you with some of the most common and important terms.

ADS MANAGER: A Facebook advertising tool designed so advertisers can create, edit, and publish multiple ads at once and have precise control over their campaigns. You can create and run your ads, target your ads to the people you care about, set your budget, see how your ads are performing, and see your billing summary, payment history, and payment method info. You can manage multiple ads at once, import ads using Microsoft Excel, and use "search and apply" filters to find what you want to work on quickly.

FACEBOOK AD STRUCTURE

There are three parts to a Facebook ad structure: campaign, ad set, and ad.

CAMPAIGN: At the top of the structure, the campaign is where you set an overall advertising objective for the ads of this grouping. This is the "why" of your ad structure.

AD SET: A step below the campaign, the ad set is where you create the audience to which you want to target your ads. Facebook targeting options include location, gender, age, and much more. You also create a budget, set a schedule for your ads, and choose your placements. This is the "who" of your ad structure.

AD: The ad is the actual creative that will appear in front of Facebook users, including the copy, headline, images or videos, and links. This is the "what" of your ad structure.

Note: There can be multiple ad sets (with different features and settings) within a campaign, and there can be multiple ads under each ad set.

CAMPAIGN-LEVEL TERMS

BUYING TYPE: How you pay for and target ads in your campaigns. Methods include dynamic auction bidding, fixed-price bidding, and reach and frequency buying.

CAMPAIGN OBJECTIVE: The overall goal of all ads in a given campaign. Grouped under awareness, consideration, and conversion, the campaign objective sets the outcome you hope to achieve with the campaign.

AD SET-LEVEL TERMS

AUDIENCE NETWORK: Organizations and websites in agreement with Facebook to extend their ad reach. Including Audience Network typically gets you more clicks but less overall engagement on your site. It's good for raising awareness but not the best for trying to encourage appointments.

BID STRATEGY: The method your ad set uses to bid for ad placements, controlling the cost per optimization event. The two strategies are "lowest cost" and "target cost."

CONNECTIONS: A section to reach people who have a specific kind of connection to your page, app, or event. You might include everyone who likes your dealership Facebook page, exclude them, or include people whose friends like your page.

CUSTOM AUDIENCE: An audience of contacts you create or upload, either from your own CRM listings or from traffic on your website. You can target ads to these audiences or exclude them within an ad set.

DAILY BUDGET: A set amount that an ad set can spend each day it runs.

DETAILED TARGETING: Parameters in the ad set that sort your audience by either including or excluding demographics, interests, and behaviors.

LIFETIME BUDGET: A set amount that an ad set can spend across the time it is active.

LOOKALIKE AUDIENCE: A group of Facebook users determined to be similar to the members of one of your custom audiences. These are segmented by one million similar users at a time, and they should be further narrowed with other targeting.

LOWEST COST: The bid strategy designed to get you the lowest possible cost per optimization event while also spending your entire budget by the time set to run. You can add a "bid cap," which tells the maximum amount to bid for an optimization event.

OPTIMIZATION FOR AD DELIVERY: The way you want Facebook to deliver ads. This affects who sees the ads to get you the best results for the lowest cost. For example, optimizing for clicks puts you in front of people more likely to click at a low cost.

PAGE: The Facebook business profile that you are using to list the ad (and whose connection types you can use for targeting).

PLACEMENTS: Where your ads will be seen. You can toggle on and off the Facebook news feed, right column, and placements on Instagram, Audience Network, and Facebook Messenger.

TARGET COST: The bid strategy designed to achieve an average cost per optimization event as close to your cost target as possible. This strategy is available only for campaigns using the app installs, conversions, or catalog sales campaign objectives.

AD-LEVEL TERMS

CALL TO ACTION: This optional button can give a cohesive direction that the user can take next, such as "Book Now," "Learn More," "Shop Now," or "Download."

CAROUSEL: An ad featuring two or more cards that may have different images, links, and ad copy. These allow you to display multiple vehicles, inventories, or services, and they let the user scroll through to find the best fit for their needs.

COLLECTION: These catalog ads pull in the inventory from your website and put it on Facebook for mobile users to scroll through, linking directly to vehicles. Copy for each vehicle can be populated with vehicle information, like price, drivetrain, etc.

EXISTING POST: An organic post that is already on your page and can be pulled in to serve as an ad. Public likes, comments, and shares will also be pulled in when the post is promoted.

DISPLAY LINK: The link shown in the bottom-left corner of an ad. This can be different from the website URL to offer a cleaner link (e.g. displaying *9clouds.com* vs. *9clouds.com/automotive-marketing-case-studies/digital-marketing-on-facebook*).

HEADLINE: Appearing below imagery, this larger text lets the user know what to expect if they click on or engage with your ad.

NEWS FEED LINK DESCRIPTION: This text is automatically pulled in from your website URL's meta description, but you can alter it to be accommodating text for the main text and headline. Remember, this usually shows only on desktop feeds, so you don't want any info here that is integral to the ad.

TEXT: The body of your ad copy, where the message will display. Think of this as the portion where your description would go on a normal Facebook post.

TRACKING: This section lets you manage tracking integrations with App Events, URL parameters to feed information to Google Analytics, your Facebook pixel, and Offline Events.

URL PARAMETERS: This is where you can drop your UTM tag string for Google Analytics, something like *utm_source=facebook&utm_medium=cpc&utm_campaign=newtrucks*. (Visit *ga-dev-tools.appspot.com/campaign-url-builder* for help building your UTM string.)

WEBSITE URL: The link to which your ad directs Facebook users when they click.

FACEBOOK AD METRICS

Facebook offers many different metrics with which to measure your ads' success.

AMOUNT SPENT: The estimated total amount of money you've spent on your campaign, ad set, or ad during its schedule.

BUDGET: The total amount of money available to your campaign, ad set, or ad.

CLICKS (ALL): The number of clicks on your ads, including clicks to your Facebook page, clicks on the "share" button, and other interactions with the ad container.

COST PER RESULT: The average amount spent for each intended outcome.

CPC (ALL): The average cost for each click, including clicks that aren't to your destination URL.

CPC (COST PER LINK CLICK): The average cost per each link click.

CPM: The average cost per 1,000 impressions.

CTR (ALL): The percentage of times people saw your ad and performed a click anywhere within the ad container.

CTR (LINK CLICK-THROUGH RATE): The percentage of times people saw your ad and performed a link click.

DELIVERY: The present status of your campaign, ad set, or ad.

ENDS: The end date for your campaign, ad set, or ad.

IMPRESSIONS: The number of times your ad was on screen.

LINK CLICKS: The number of clicks on ad links to select destinations or experiences, on or off Facebook-owned properties.

OFFLINE EVENTS: This tool lets you get a conservative estimate of how your ads are impacting return on investment (ROI) by measuring how many of your leads or recent buyers saw your Facebook ads. This works by uploading spreadsheets of basic contact information, which Facebook cross-references with those who engaged with your ads.

REACH: The number of people who saw your ad at least once. Reach is different from impressions, which may include multiple views of your ad by the same people.

RESULTS: The number of times your ad achieved an outcome, based on the objective and settings you selected.

SCHEDULE: The date range over which an ad set is running.

SETTING UP FACEBOOK

A professional Facebook account needs a solid foundation. To take advantage of the best that Facebook, and this field guide, have to offer, you will want a complete setup. This section will get you started.

Facebook often changes, so for specific and the most updated how-to steps, take our online course, Facebook Set-Up for Pros, at 9clouds.com/facebook/education.

> *Facebook frequently updates its interface and continually offers new audiences and features. Sign up for free updates to this book as we add recipes and keep up with the latest Facebook features at 9clouds.com/facebook/fieldguide.*

1. HOW TO SET UP FACEBOOK BUSINESS MANAGER FOR A DEALERSHIP

For any dealership, 9 Clouds recommends using Facebook Business Manager for creating, analyzing, and budgeting for Facebook ads.

This free tool is especially useful for teams with multiple people because the administrator can manage the access and permissions for other employees all in one place.

Facebook Business Manager is your home base for professional Facebook ads. It enables you to manage everything, including multiple pages, multiple users, multiple partners, and more. Plus, it allows you to quickly see analytics from one or more accounts.

We recommend setting up a Facebook Business Manager for your business. If you have multiple stores within that business, each one will get its own page and ad account, but they will all live under one Business Manager.

It is possible to have multiple Business Managers, but we recommend that only if you have separate businesses.

To set up your Business Manager account, visit *business.facebook.com*.

Pro tip: You do not need to have a personal Facebook account to create a Facebook Business Manager.

Once you have set up your Business Manager account, continue to step two.

SET UP YOUR ACCOUNT AT *business.facebook.com*.

2. HOW TO SET UP A FACEBOOK PAGE FOR A DEALERSHIP

Now that you have Facebook Business Manager ready to go, visit **Business Settings**, and choose **People and Assets**. Click **Pages** and **+ Add**.

There, you can add a page you already own, request access to a page, or create a brand-new page.

> *Pro tip: If you are already an admin on the page, when you click **Add a Page**, it will automatically be approved. If you request access, the admin of the page will have to click their notifications (the globe icon) and approve the request.*

A Facebook page is your business' home base on Facebook. A page is most known as the place where you post updates and comments.

When you run an ad, the ad does not show up on your Facebook page. The ad shows which page is running the ad.

Your page's icon shows up on the top-left corner of an ad and is required to run an ad. A page can also help target ads by showing ads to only people who like your page or friends of people who like your page.

When creating an ad in Business Manager, you can choose which page will run the ad.

Use multiple page roles to allow agencies or employees to place ads without controlling all aspects of your business' page.

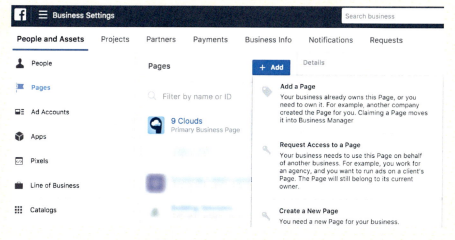

SET UP YOUR DEALERSHIP'S FACEBOOK PAGE WITHIN BUSINESS MANAGER.

3. HOW TO SET UP A FACEBOOK AD ACCOUNT

Now that your Facebook page is up and running, return to the Business Settings page within Business Manager, and choose **People and Assets**. Click **Ad Accounts** and + **Add**.

There, you can add an ad account you already own, request access to an ad account, or create a brand-new ad account.

> *Pro tip: Every ad account has a payment method, such as a credit card. Only create multiple ad accounts if you need to seperate billing between stores or departments.*

A Facebook ad account is where all of the ads are created and paid.

Every ad account has a method of payment, such as a credit card or PayPal. You can also choose your currency for an ad account.

There is a limit to the number of ad accounts one Business Manager can have. To avoid hitting your limit, only create new ad accounts if you need to seperate billing between rooftops or departments.

Keeping your ads within a single ad account is also beneficial because it allows you to easily duplicate, edit, pause, and restart ads. Ads created in different ad accounts are not easily shared.

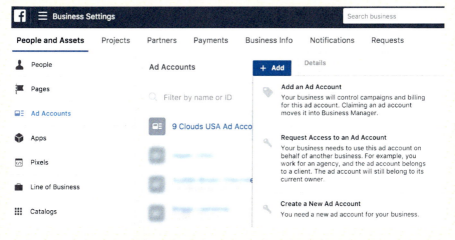

SET UP YOUR DEALERSHIP'S AD ACCOUNT WITHIN BUSINESS MANAGER.

4. HOW TO SET UP A FACEBOOK PIXEL

The Facebook pixel is your eyes and ears on your website. With the pixel, you are able to advertise to people who visit your website and take specific action, such as visiting a certain page. The pixel also allows you to set up dynamic retargeting ads, so your visitors see the exact vehicle they visited on your website.

What makes Facebook a powerful source of advertising is that all of the information gathered by pixels across the web is shared with Facebook. That means that you can target likely car buyers. Facebook knows who is a likely car buyer because they are visiting multiple dealer websites.

> *Pro tip: Pixel installation requires technical knowledge of the code on your website. If you're not comfortable adding it, ask for help!*

A Facebook pixel needs to first be set up within your Facebook Business Manager. Click the three lines (the "hamburger"), and choose **Events Manager** under the **Measure and Report** column. Then choose **Add Data Source > Facebook Pixel**, and follow the instructions.

After the pixel is created, it needs to be installed on your website. We recommend installing the Facebook pixel using Google Tag Manager, so you can easily edit and update the pixel without going through your web provider. Visit *google.com/tagmanager* to get started.

Create a Facebook Pixel   ×

Create a Facebook pixel to measure results from your advertising, optimize ads for conversions, and build audiences for remarketing. Learn more.

Pixel Name   9 Clouds   42

You can create up to 10 pixels with your business account.

By clicking create, I agree to the Facebook pixel terms.   **Give Feedback**   **Cancel**   **Create**

SET UP YOUR DEALERSHIP'S PIXEL WITHIN BUSINESS MANAGER.

5. HOW TO SET UP A FACEBOOK PRODUCT CATALOG

If you can run only one ad on Facebook, make it an inventory ad.

Inventory ads show the vehicles you have on the lot to people shopping for those vehicles. In order to set up inventory ads and dynamic retargeting ads, you will need a Facebook catalog.

The Facebook catalog connects with your inventory feed. When you get new inventory, it shows up automatically in the Facebook catalog. When you sell a vehicle, Facebook removes it from the catalog.

Within the catalog, you can create product sets to filter your inventory by price, body style, mileage, and more. Then, your inventory ads can dynamically show any vehicles that fit your filtering criteria.

The best part of these inventory ads is that they are dynamic. They automatically update based on your inventory, so there is less management for your marketing team.

> Pro tip: Build multiple product sets within your Facebook catalog. This allows you to create inventory ads showing specific types of inventory based on brand, mileage, price, etc.

A Facebook catalog requires an inventory feed. The feed can be dynamically pulled from your inventory provider or can be uploaded manually. To make this process easier, we developed Cumulus, which will do all of the work for you. Learn more at 9clouds.com/facebook.

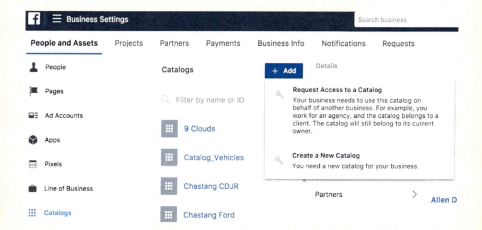

SET UP YOUR DEALERSHIP'S INVENTORY FEED WITHIN BUSINESS MANAGER.

6. HOW TO SET UP AND INTEGRATE AN INSTAGRAM ACCOUNT

Instagram is a photo-based social network that is owned by Facebook. Shockingly, Instagram has 70% higher engagement than Facebook![3] Plus, Instagram has more than 800 million users of its own.

Marketing on Instagram requires visually stunning ads that make users want to stop scrolling and take action. By default, Facebook will place your ads in Instagram. We recommend Instagram ads only if your ads are eye-catching.

The best way to decide how to advertise on Instagram is to first set up an Instagram account and view the photos and videos posted on the site.

Also look at the Instagram "Stories," which are a series of images that do not stay up on someone's account. Car and RV dealers can use the Stories feature to advertise, or tell a story, with a series of images of videos.

> *Pro tip: Facebook ads can be shown on Instagram without an Instagram account and will be displayed as the Facebook page.*

First, create an Instagram account on *instagram.com* or via the Instagram app. Then, in your Facebook Business Manager, visit **Business Settings**, and choose **People and Assets**. Click **Instagram Accounts** and + **Add**. There, you can enter your Instagram username and password. You can also assign the Instagram account to a Facebook ad account or a partner.

[3] https://locowise.com/blog/instagram-engagement-rate-is-higher-than-facebook

Add an Instagram Account for Advertising

Enter the username and password for your Instagram account.

Username

Password

Step 1 of 2

Cancel   Next

When you add the account you agree to Facebook's Terms and Pages Terms.

SET UP YOUR DEALERSHIP'S INSTAGRAM ACCOUNT WITHIN BUSINESS MANAGER.

7. HOW TO SET UP FACEBOOK OFFLINE EVENTS

The most common question with Facebook advertising is "Is it worth it?" The best way to know is by using Offline Events.

Offline Events tell you if a lead or a sale viewed a Facebook ad before becoming a lead or before purchasing. Facebook matches your lead/sale email or phone number from your CRM with the emails/phone numbers of people who viewed your ads. Typically, we see more than 80% of the contacts in a car dealer's CRM match with users on Facebook.

> *Pro tip: Offline Events are not "de-duped." That means that if you upload all sales from January and later upload sales from January and February, the January sales are counted twice. Set a specific time, like once a month, to upload your Offline Events. This will ensure clean data.*

Facebook then compares the time and date of the lead/sale with the time and date of when they saw an ad. If they saw an ad before they became a lead or purchased, it is an offline conversion.

Facebook Offline Events not only tell you how many people saw an ad before taking action, they also can tell you the value of those actions. You can upload the revenue or income from each sale, and Facebook will tell you how much money you made. This makes it easy to calculate the return on investment (ROI) of a campaign. If you spent less on the campaign than you made from the campaign, you have positive ROI.

Create an Offline Event Set   ✕

Create an offline event set to use for uploading and managing data related to offline activities you want to track, measure, optimize ads for, and market against.

You can upload data files to this set once you've created it.

Name

Choose a name for your offline event set

Description

Add an optional description

By clicking Create, you agree to Offline Conversions Terms.   Cancel   Create

CREATE YOUR OFFLINE EVENTS SET UNDER THE EVENTS MANAGER IN THE MAIN MENU.

Click the three lines (the "hamburger"), and choose **Events Manager** under the **Measure and Report** column. Then choose **Add Data Source > Facebook Offline Event,** and follow the instructions. Make sure that it is chosen as the default Offline Event for your ad account, so all of your ads are automatically measured.

After the Offline Event is created, you will need to import your lead and sales data into your Facebook Offline Event via a .CSV file. Visit our training video at *9clouds.com/live* to learn more.

8. HOW TO SET UP FACEBOOK LEAD ACCESS

Facebook Lead Ads are a powerful way to grow your database without leads having to visit your website. They see an ad on Facebook and fill out a form on Facebook, and the information they provide can be sent to your CRM.

To make sure these leads are delivered to your CRM, you will want to set up Facebook Lead Access.

Once your CRM is connected, either directly or through a tool like Zapier or LeadsBridge, you can manage who can view those leads from your Facebook Business Manager.

> *Pro tip: Not all CRMs are integrated, but other tools (such as Zapier or LeadsBridge) can often do the work for you. Take our online course, Facebook Set-Up for Pros, at* 9clouds.com/facebook/education.

Within your Facebook Business Manager, visit **Business Settings**, and choose **People and Assets**. Click **Leads Access**. There, you can choose who has access to leads.

You will also need to connect a CRM to your page. Visit your Facebook page, and click **Publishing Tools**. On the left side, choose **Leads Setup**, and follow the instructions.

| Page | Inbox | Appointments | Notifications 2 | Insights | **Publishing Tools** | | Settings | Help ▾ |

Sounds •
Sound Collection

Connecting to a CRM

You need an existing CRM account to connect a CRM to your lead ads. If you aren't using a CRM, visit the **CRM integrations page** to see some of the CRMs that are currently supported, or visit the **Help Center**.

Jobs
Job Applications

> **Step 1: Find Your CRM**

Lead Ads Forms
Forms Library
Draft Forms Library

> **Step 2: Connect to Your CRM**

| **Leads Setup**

> **Step 3: Manage Your Leads**

SET UP YOUR DEALERSHIP'S LEAD ACCESS WITHIN BUSINESS MANAGER.

9. HOW TO SET UP PEOPLE AND PARTNERS

One of the most complex and important roles of Business Manager is managing who has access to what. There are two ways to easily assign assets and permissions: People and Partners.

People is when you add a single individual, such as an employee. You can choose which pages and accounts they have access to, and you can quickly remove them from everything with a single click.

Partners is when you are adding a company. They may want to add their own employees and staff to specific pages or ad accounts. You don't have to manage this process for them. Instead, add them as a partner using their business ID. The business ID is long string of numbers found in the URL, or web address, after **...business_id=**. The partner will have to log in to their Business Manager and tell you what their business ID is for you to get started.

When adding a partner, you are able to quickly check all the assets the partner should have access to. If you stop working with the partner, you can easily remove them, and all of their access will be revoked.

> *Pro tip: When adding a partner, you can provide access to all assets in one simple screen. That means you can check boxes for the pages, ad accounts, pixels, etc. that you want them to have access to. This is the fastest way to get someone started with managing your Facebook advertising.*

Use the People and Partners features to help others quickly scale your Facebook marketing efforts.

Add A New Partner
Setup

Add a new partner to allow them to access assets your business owns. While they will have access to use them, your business will still be in control of the asset.

Partner Business ID

Cancel   Next

SET UP YOUR DEALERSHIP'S PEOPLE AND PARTNERS WITHIN BUSINESS MANAGER.

Within your Facebook Business Manager, visit **Business Settings**, and choose **People and Assets** or **Partners**.

People is perfect if you are adding a single individual. Partners is the best choice if you want a marketing agency or technology vendor to be able to add its own staff after you give its company access.

TARGETING ON FACEBOOK

Facebook enables ad targeting based on three types of data.

DATA TYPE #1: FACEBOOK DATA

Facebook users share data through their profile. A user's birthday, education, address, gender, and much more are all data points that advertisers can use.

Additionally, Facebook tracks a user's engagement on Facebook and web pages running the Facebook pixel, including (but not limited to):

- Facebook pages they like
- Photos they share
- People they interact with on Facebook
- Web pages they visit
- Their current location when they use Facebook on a mobile device

This engagement provides additional ways that advertisers can find their ideal customers.

DATA TYPE #2: THIRD-PARTY DATA

Facebook not only has access to data *it* gathers. It also purchases data from other data harvesters to provide more ways to target advertisements.

Most importantly for auto dealers, Facebook has access to Polk data in the United States, so dealers can target owners of specific vehicle makes. Facebook also purchases data from Equifax to target ads based on economic information. Other data providers gather information from loyalty programs at grocery stores and gas stations, plus information on people who use credit cards to make purchases at local auto repair shops.

> Many audiences based on this third-party data is publicly available on Facebook. However, additional automotive audiences are available to partners. Visit 9clouds.com/facebook to get started.

By request, dealerships can gain access to these effective automotive audiences:

- In-market shoppers at the model level (e.g. in-market Honda CR-V shoppers or Ford Escape shoppers)
- In-market pre-owned shoppers at the make level (e.g. in-market used Ford or used Chevrolet shoppers)
- Visa and Mastercard segments across fixed ops, including transaction data from independent service and repair shops, dealership service and repair, parts and accessories, or tires

DATA TYPE #3: YOUR DATA

The best advertisers on Facebook combine Facebook and third-party data with their own data, usually pulled from the CRM. On Facebook, advertisers can target ads to specific audiences based on email addresses or phone numbers.

Popular audiences for car dealers include (but are not limited to):

- Past customers
- Leads who haven't purchased
- Customers whose lease is nearing completion
- Buyers who haven't serviced in six months
- Customers nearing two years after purchase (to comply with Canadian spam laws)
- Service customers who refused recommended service

By pulling specific segments from your CRM and importing into a Facebook custom audience, you can run Facebook ads more targeted than competitors who do not have access to your CRM data.

BUDGETING ON FACEBOOK

The most common question about Facebook ads that we hear at 9 Clouds is "How much should I spend on Facebook?"

The ideal Facebook ad budget should be based on three things:
1. *A percentage of your overall digital ad spend*
2. *Your audience size*
3. *The goal of your ad campaigns*

The Facebook Rule of One is based on our experience working with car dealers and automotive marketers. It translates these three criteria into a simple budgeting formula:

- 1/3rd of your entire digital ad budget should be spent on Facebook.
- $1 per day for every 1,000 people in your audience is a good starting budget.
- 1 ad campaign should showcase your inventory to in-market buyers.

BUDGETING TIP #1: ARRANGE YOUR ALLOCATION

The first principle relates to your overall budget. If you are spending $9,000 per month on Google AdWords, we recommend you shift at least $3,000 of that to Facebook. We typically see clicks on Facebook costing a quarter to a third of the amount they would cost on Google. That means shifting some of your budget to Facebook will increase the traffic to your site and also help you increase awareness of your store and inventory.

Google is the "what," and Facebook is the "who." On Google, people are searching for something, such as "best F-150 near me." On Facebook, you are targeting a type of person, such as 30- to 40-year-olds who like hunting and own a truck. On Facebook, the people to whom you are showing ads may not be searching for a vehicle *yet*, so you are trying to make them aware of your store before they search from someone else.

THE FACEBOOK RULE OF ONE.

BUDGETING TIP #2: MIRROR THE AUDIENCE

The second principle helps you identify a budget that fits your target audience. It highlights an important lesson that the bigger your audience, the more expensive it will be to get in front of them. Hopefully, this principle should help you target your ideal audience, so you don't waste budget on people who are not your customers.

As an example, if you are trying to market to people who live within 20 miles of your store and are likely to buy in the next three months, Facebook might calculate that there are 20,000 people who fit this criteria. The Facebook Rule of One would say you should spend at least $20 per day to reach at least 80% of this audience one to two times (known as frequency).

Doubling this spend to $2 per day for every 1,000 people will typically increase your frequency to two to four times per month. This is the sweet spot of reaching the most people for the lowest cost. We recommend a frequency of at least three for your most important audiences.

BUDGETING TIP #3: INVEST IN INVENTORY

The third principle highlights a simple truth about advertising in general: you should show cars to people who want to buy cars.

We have found that dynamic inventory ads, where the photos and vehicles featured update automatically based on your inventory, have three times higher engagement and click-through rates (CTRs) than regular ads. What's more, these ads can be set up as retargeting ads, so they show people who have visited your site the exact vehicle they were looking at. If you sell the vehicle, the ad shuts off.

> *If you can choose only one campaign to run, run an inventory ad. If you want the ad to run automatically, we have a tool called Cumulus that can help. Visit 9clouds.com/facebook/cumulus to get started.*

Cumulus connects your inventory feed to your Facebook Business Manager, so you can launch ads that convert and do not require ongoing management.

If you have a small inventory, you can update your photos and featured vehicles on a regular basis. That way, you still get the benefit of showing vehicles to people likely to purchase.

AD FORMATS

Facebook offers seven unique ad formats for
businesses to promote their products and services.
Each format has unique benefits and purposes,
so we identified the most appropriate formats
for each campaign included in this book.

CAROUSEL

The most commonly deployed format at our agency is the **carousel**, which shows several images, or "tiles," in a rotating format. Users can easily swipe to the left to view the series of images and their corresponding links.

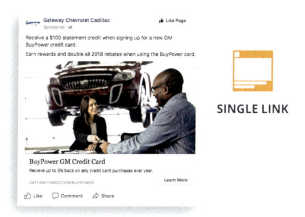

SINGLE LINK

Single link ads, also known as photo ads, are the simplest and most familiar Facebook ad format. As the name implies, these ads are a great way to feature photos of your store or staff. They're also the easiest type of ad to construct.

VIDEO

Similar in style to single link ads, **video ads** are a captivating way to feature TV spots or other recordings from your dealership. Video ads also feature a link to a relevant landing page, where people can explore more.

COLLECTION

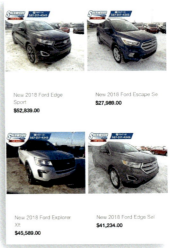

Collection ads are a relatively new full-screen format that allows dealers to display several vehicles in "product sets." Each image links directly to the corresponding vehicle detail page (VDP) on the dealer's website. This format requires an inventory feed connected with a Facebook catalog within Facebook Business Manager.

Facebook's new toy!

LEAD FORM

Facebook knows more about us than most of us would prefer, but this data is incredibly useful for advertisers. The **lead form** format pre-fills with known values, such as first name and email address. You can also ask people to fill out custom fields for things like trade evaluations or appointment scheduling. This format requires a "bridge" integration to bring the data from Facebook into your CRM.

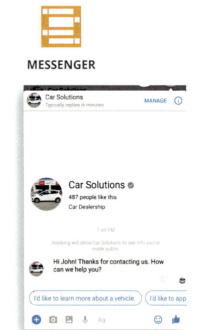

Answer questions. Schedule appointments. Convert leads! **Messenger** ads are a relatively new ad format that allows dealerships to connect and communicate with customers in a meaningful way. This is a great ad format for sparking new conversations about your products and services. Dealerships can also suggest pre-filled messages for the user.

AD FORMAT ICONS

Look for these icons on each recipe in the following sections.

CAROUSEL

COLLECTION

SINGLE LINK

LEAD FORM

VIDEO

MESSENGER

ABOUT THE RECIPES IN THIS BOOK

The ideas, tactics, and tips on the following pages are real-world examples from our work with auto dealers in North America. We designed the recipes to be easy to read and use for your dealership.

This icon indicates the recipe's placement in your overall strategy (top, middle, or bottom of the funnel).

These four icons show the suggested ad format, platforms, time frame, and difficulty of each recipe.

This sidebar shows the suggested targeting parameters for the campaign. These include automotive audiences (built into Facebook), custom audiences (lists of people from your CRM), or third-party audiences from special integrations.

Our crew is confident in the quality of these campaigns, so we decided to put our names on 'em.

QUALIFY USED VEHICLE SHOPPERS

CAROUSEL FORMAT   **MOBILE & DESKTOP**   **RUN UP TO 3 MONTHS**   **SET-UP DIFFICULTY**

RECOMMENDED AUDIENCES

- In-market used vehicle shoppers

- People who registered used vehicles two or more years ago

- A custom audience of CRM contacts who purchased used vehicles two or more years ago

- Unqualified/unknown used vehicle leads from your CRM

The main goal for any top-of-funnel Facebook ad is to figure out who the heck might be interested in your vehicles. Engagement is the name of the game here.

The carousel format is important at this stage, because it allows you to show several "buckets" of vehicles into which people can click and thereby self-segment.

Aside from SRP traffic (measured as clicks in Facebook or visits in Google Analytics), keep an eye on click-through rate, since you want as much engagement as possible for segmentation. Also, a low CPC here will allow you to stretch your ad budget to a wider audience.

 RACHEL SPEISER

SECTION 1: TOP-OF-FUNNEL ADS

The view from the top is wide. At this young phase in your Facebook advertising strategy, it's important to keep an open mind — and a clear "open" sign on your digital door.

In many cases, people at the top of the funnel have never heard of you and are simply discovering the problems they want to solve. For example, that college grad is probably going to need an economical sedan for her new daily commute. Just down the street, you might have parents who are expecting their third child and suddenly need a third-row SUV.

These contexts are the framework around which you can build a relevant, empathetic message, introducing your brand as the authority around the available solutions.

Let's dive in!

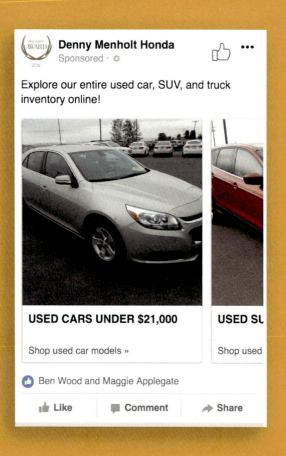

QUALIFY USED VEHICLE SHOPPERS

CAROUSEL FORMAT

MOBILE & DESKTOP

RUN UP TO 3 MONTHS

SETUP DIFFICULTY

RECOMMENDED AUDIENCES

- In-market used vehicle shoppers

- People who registered used vehicles two or more years ago

- A custom audience of CRM contacts who purchased used vehicles two or more years ago

- Unqualified/unknown used vehicle leads from your CRM

The main goal for any top-of-funnel Facebook ad is to figure out who the heck might be interested in your vehicles. Engagement is the name of the game here.

The carousel format is important at this stage because it allows you to show several "buckets" of vehicles into which people can click and thereby self-segment.

Aside from search results page (SRP) traffic (measured as clicks in Facebook or visits in Google Analytics), keep an eye on CTR, since you want as much engagement as possible for segmentation. Also, a low cost per click (CPC) will allow you to stretch your ad budget to a wider audience.

RACHEL SPEISER

REACH SHOPPERS JUST DOWN THE ROAD

 CAROUSEL FORMAT

 MOBILE & DESKTOP

 RUN UP TO 1 MONTH

 SETUP DIFFICULTY

RECOMMENDED AUDIENCES

- Used vehicle shoppers in neighboring cities or geographic areas

- People in neighboring areas who registered used vehicles two or more years ago

- A custom audience of CRM service contacts who live in neighboring areas

Targeting in-market shoppers within the vicinity of your dealership seems like a no-brainer. But have you considered trying to capture top-of-funnel leads just a little farther away?

To increase brand awareness, this dealership in Butte, Montana, showed ads to residents of the nearby city of Anaconda. It features a simple carousel of available models — and explains that Butte is only a short drive away — relating to a whole new host of car shoppers.

This strategy is all about brand awareness, so focus on high-level metrics like reach, CTR, and CPC. You're aiming to reach as many (qualified!) shoppers as possible for as low a cost as possible.

SARAH KLONGERBO

BID FOR BUDGETED BUYERS

CAROUSEL FORMAT **MOBILE & DESKTOP** **RUN UP TO 1 MONTH** **SETUP DIFFICULTY**

RECOMMENDED AUDIENCES

- People who registered used vehicles two or more years ago
- Unqualified in-market used vehicle shoppers
- A custom audience of unqualified or unknown used vehicle leads from your CRM

Offering price tiers on used vehicles helps top-of-funnel marketing to understand where shoppers fall in price range. Many shoppers are looking for price first, then things like body style and brand of vehicle.

Using the carousel card option offers viewers a selection of choices to assist in pulling them down the funnel of car shopping. Share a variety of vehicles throughout the carousel cards to show the large inventory you offer.

After running this ad, you can then remarket with other campaigns targeted to the people who clicked on the various body style cards in the carousel.

 BETSY SPRENKLE

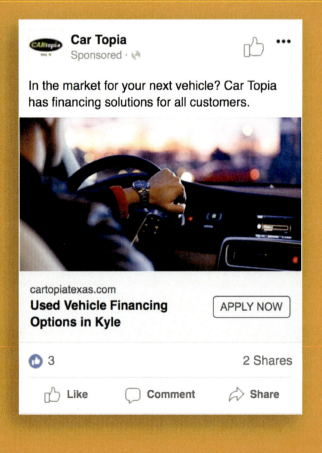

PUT FINANCING FIRST

SINGLE LINK FORMAT   **MOBILE & DESKTOP**   **RUN UP TO 1 MONTH**   **SETUP DIFFICULTY**

RECOMMENDED AUDIENCES

- In-market used vehicle shoppers in lower income brackets

- Used vehicle shoppers with multiple lines of credit (who are most likely to benefit from financing solutions)

- A lookalike audience based on a list of similar sales from your CRM

Once you find the people who may be interested buying from you, it's time to identify priorities.

One effective way to make yourself known is to communicate how your business differs from your competition. What experience do you provide that others don't? To boost used sales, Car Topia highlighted its commitment to offering financing solutions for everyone.

Inventory isn't always a priority for shoppers, so make it clear what else makes your dealership a great fit for your audience. That will give them an opportunity to continue down the sales funnel.

JADEN MILLER

Major World Chrysler Jeep Dodge Ram
Sponsored ·

Why do New Yorkers trust Major CDJR for their vehicle needs? We've got 5 reasons. 👇

1. Our Values of Honesty, Integrity, and Reliability

2. Latest Jeep, & R

 Like   Comment   Share

TELL YOUR STORY (WITHOUT THE CARS)

| CAROUSEL FORMAT | MOBILE & DESKTOP | RUN UP TO 1 MONTH | SETUP DIFFICULTY |

RECOMMENDED AUDIENCES

- People who registered certain brands of used vehicles two or more years ago

- In-market used vehicle shoppers who are looking for certain brands

- A lookalike audience based on a list of past sales from your CRM

In order to persuade people to purchase the latest car, truck, or SUV on your lot, you need to show them why they should buy from you. Think of this ad as your dealership's elevator pitch.

Dealership branding ads can take many forms. No matter what, they should highlight what makes your dealership different from others, linking to landing pages or blog posts that further explain the points on the cards.

This ad gives those who may soon be or are already in the market for a vehicle a good idea of what your dealership is all about.

 JACQUELYN JACOBSMA

SHOW YOUR STORY (WITHOUT THE CARS)

VIDEO FORMAT   **MOBILE & DESKTOP**   **RUN UP TO 1 MONTH**   **SETUP DIFFICULTY**

RECOMMENDED AUDIENCES

- People who registered certain brands of used vehicles two or more years ago
- In-market used vehicle shoppers who are looking for certain brands
- A lookalike audience based on a list of past sales from your CRM

With tier-one and tier-two efforts already promoting products and incentives, your biggest challenge is showing a lead why they want to buy a new vehicle from your store.

This video ad promotes your store's brand, reaching people early in the buyer's journey and planting a seed that *your* store is the good one.

A 15- to 30-second video gives you the space to convey your story. You can then follow up with people who clicked to your website from this video with a middle-of-funnel ad. Because attention spans are increasingly short, put the most important information in the first few seconds.

MATT STOFFEL

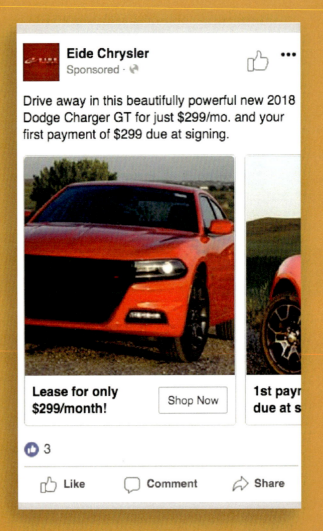

USE GREAT PHOTOS FOR GREAT CARS

 CAROUSEL FORMAT

 MOBILE & DESKTOP

 RUN UP TO 1 MONTH

 SETUP DIFFICULTY

RECOMMENDED AUDIENCES

- Brand owners, new vehicle shoppers, or near-market shoppers (new or used)

- People who are actively shopping in the segment of a certain body style

- Third-party targeting for shoppers of a certain model

As it turns out, the Dodge Charger is not the most popular vehicle in North Dakota (that title officially belongs to the F-150). However, a few boutique images, combined with an attractive lease offer, made this Charger turn more heads online.

In our experience, most vehicle listings suffer from stale, boring, and sometimes even blurry images, which are easy to ignore. Taking the time to procure high-quality images pays off in attention.

When Eide Chrysler wanted to highlight its Dodge Charger offers, we peppered this carousel with images of the Charger in the North Dakotan countryside for local flavor.

 JOHN NELSON

SECTION 2: MIDDLE-OF-FUNNEL ADS

Now that you've introduced your inventory and brand to your audience, it's time to take the next step toward a sale.

At this phase in your Facebook advertising strategy, put your knowledge to work.

In many cases, people at the middle of the funnel have already heard of your store and are weighing their options. For example, now that the college grad knows she wants to lease a small SUV, you have an opportunity to show her the selection at your dealership. And now that the family of four has had their SUV for a few years, they might be interested in an upgrade.

These contexts are the framework around which you can build a helpful, educational message and reinforce your authority with great timing.

HIGHLIGHT THEIR NEIGHBORS

CAROUSEL FORMAT   **MOBILE & DESKTOP**   **RUN UP TO 1 MONTH**   **SETUP DIFFICULTY**

RECOMMENDED AUDIENCES

- A custom audience of unsold leads from your CRM who are interested in a certain model

- A retargeting audience of people who have viewed pages on your website featuring a certain model

- Third-party targeting for active shoppers of a certain model

Leads in the middle of the funnel are ready to buy a vehicle — but they still need to decide which model they want. That's where a feature-rich, model-specific Facebook ad comes in handy.

If you're trying to promote a specific model in your inventory — as this Nissan dealership was aiming to promote its new Titan inventory — try a carousel ad targeted to those in the market for that model, displaying its most fabulous features.

To really hit home, make the ad personal and specific to your area. This store, for instance, interviewed a local Titan owner, wrote a blog post about it, and linked to the Q&A in the carousel ad.

SARAH KLONGERBO

Lexus of Calgary
Sponsored

Come see us when you're ready for a test drive!

Used 2013 Lexus GS 450h

$34,721.00

Used 201

$44,921.00

 Like   Comment   Share

MAINTAIN BROWSING MOMENTUM

CAROUSEL FORMAT   **MOBILE & DESKTOP**   **RUN UP TO 3 MONTHS**   **SETUP DIFFICULTY**

RECOMMENDED AUDIENCES

- People who have browsed new vehicle VDPs in the last 15-30 days

- People who have browsed used vehicle VDPs in the last 7-10 days

INTEGRATIONS

- Facebook pixel

- Cumulus (by 9 Clouds)

A dynamic catalog retargeting ad is excellent for appealing to consumers at the middle of the funnel who are already taking action on your website.

The carousel will pull in a custom selection of inventory, based on each online vehicle shopper's activity.

Consider the number of actions it takes for a consumer to buy a vehicle before setting the number of days for the retargeting ad to appear. Google has determined that the average in-market auto shopper makes 24 actions before actually purchasing. Nineteen of these 24 touchpoints are part of the digital car sales funnel.

RACHEL SPEISER

ILLUSTRATE OPPORTUNITY

CAROUSEL FORMAT   **MOBILE & DESKTOP**   **RUN UP TO 2 MONTHS**   **SETUP DIFFICULTY**

RECOMMENDED AUDIENCES

- A retargeting audience of people who have viewed any new model VDPs within the last 15 days

- A retargeting audience of people who have viewed new model SRPs within the last 30 days

- Third-party targeting for relevant models

Just because someone has viewed a new vehicle on your website doesn't necessarily mean they know the opportunities to buy (or lease) it at a great price. This recipe maintains your new VDP traffic and guides visitors down the path toward a sale.

When Major Chrysler wanted us to create a full-funnel advertising strategy, we made sure to include this evergreen ad, which brings qualified shoppers back to regularly updated specials pages.

Bringing attention to your specials allows your dealership to channel tier-two incentives and further qualify your visitors for the next stage of the funnel.

JOHN NELSON

Eide Ford Lincoln
Sponsored ·

This New 2018 Ford Explorer offer won't last long!

🔵 Lease for $439/mo. [36 months w/ first payment only due at signing - includes security deposit.]

🔵 Buy for $33,490 [Over $4,000 off MSRP!]

*Offer ends 2/5/18

See All New Ford Explorers in Bismarck

  8   5 Comments   2 Shares

 Like   Comment   Share

FLEX YOUR SELECTION

 COLLECTION FORMAT

 MOBILE PLACEMENT

 RUN UP TO 1 MONTH

5/10 SETUP DIFFICULTY

RECOMMENDED AUDIENCES
- A retargeting audience of website visitors who view landing pages, SRPs, or VDPs for a certain model
- Third-party targeting for active shoppers of a certain brand
- A custom audience of unsold leads from your CRM who are interested in a certain model

INTEGRATIONS
- Cumulus (By 9 Clouds)

A middle-of-funnel ad works to align a buyer's needs to relevant products and move the right people closer to purchasing. You can then build and monitor their purchase intent, moving them closer to becoming a customer.

A full-page canvas or collection ad for mobile not only looks great, but also shows the full inventory of a certain product. This ad was targeted to in-market Explorer/SUV shoppers, so if a customer is in the market for something else, this ad won't waste their time and your dollars. The beauty of this ad is that by showing it to the right people, it moves them further along in the funnel. Once a lead clicks on the ad and views the SRP or a VDP, you can then show them a retargeting ad.

 JADEN MILLER

Porsche South Bay
Sponsored

Stop dreaming. Start shopping.

As a Porsche Premier Dealer for 5 consecutive years with 300+ Porsches in stock, there's no better place to start shopping.

Our sales and service staff live and breathe the Porsche (and even race Porsche's on our days off!).

Come see, touch and drive your next dream car.

porschesouthbay.com
LA South Bay's Porsche Leader

SHOP NOW

 Like   Comment   Share

RELATE INVENTORY TO INTERESTS

SINGLE LINK   **MOBILE PLACEMENT**   **RUN UP TO 1 MONTH**   **SETUP DIFFICULTY**

RECOMMENDED AUDIENCES

- Work- or lifestyle-related categories

- People who are interested in a certain model (using the **Interests** menu)

- Third-party targeting for active shoppers of a certain model

- A lookalike audience based on a list of model sales from your CRM

Marketing to a niche audience can bring a high ROI at a low CPC with the right targeting. In this ad, we marketed a sale on Corvettes to a highly targeted audience.

We often prefer to use behavioral targeting over interest targeting — but when we're making ads for specific vehicles (like Porches, Mustangs, or even Jeeps), interest-based targeting wins.

Facebook's interest-based targeting looks at users who share, follow, and post about their favorite interests. These audiences are already engaged and highly likely to click and convert on the ad. A relevance score over six and CPC under $0.50 is ideal for this group.

BETSY SPRENKLE

Chastang Ford
Sponsored ·

We have the best team, the best selection, and the best prices around.

Find your new Ford in Houston

More

👍 24

👍 Like   💬 Comment   ➤ Share

RETAIN SHOPPERS IN SPECIFIC SEGMENTS

 COLLECTION FORMAT

 MOBILE PLACEMENT

 RUN UP TO 6 MONTHS

4/10 SETUP DIFFICULTY

RECOMMENDED AUDIENCES

- In-market truck shoppers
- Third-party targeting for people who are interested in specific truck models
- A lookalike audience based on a list of current new truck customers from your CRM

INTEGRATIONS

- Cumulus (By 9 Clouds)

Identifying a visitor's interests can be tricky, but with the right integrations, you can retain their attention and also remain relevant over a longer period of time.

If you have a specific brand of trucks — let's say Ford — create specific collections for the current model year F-150 and the previous year F-150 (both new).

To reinforce your brand, show a banner image with your crew or your storefront.

These work really well with a large audience, but if you have time, run them to a model-specific audience for an even higher CTR.

 ALLEN DAY

 **Green Mazda**
Sponsored ·

Got questions on finding a new or used vehicle? Need service? Something else?
We've got you covered. Let us know how we can help you today.

Chat with a Member of Our Team Right Now   [SEND MESSAGE]

 Like

Green Mazda

10:26PM

You opened this conversation through an ad. When you reply, Green Mazda will see your public info and which ad you clicked.

Hi Scott! Thanks for reaching out. How can we help you?

> **Where's our store?**
>
> **Shop New Mazdas**
>
> **Shop Pre-Owned Rides**

Type a message

STRIKE UP A CONVERSATION

MESSENGER FORMAT **MOBILE PLACEMENT** **RUN UP TO 1 MONTH** **SETUP DIFFICULTY**

RECOMMENDED AUDIENCES

- A retargeting audience of people who have viewed VDPs or SRPs within the last week

- In-market shoppers for relevant brands

- Third-party targeting for the specific models on your lot

- A custom audience of unsold leads from your CRM

As we've all become more reliant on smartphones and social media, it has become less likely that a lot of people are going to pick up the phone to ask a question. Sad, right? Still, that's not your problem to fix.

Instead, a general Messenger ad provides folks with a no-hassle way to ask about your store, inventory, or anything else keeping them from buying. Having a real human ready to answer questions is a valuable tactic for engaging leads in the middle of the funnel.

With this ad, you can figure out exactly where they are in the sales funnel and move them along toward the close. Just be ready to respond quickly!

 MATT STOFFEL

SECTION 3: BOTTOM-OF-FUNNEL ADS

With helpful, brand-building education at the top and middle areas of the funnel, it's now time to convert your informed visitors into customers.

At this final phase in your Facebook advertising strategy, encourage your qualified leads to set an in-person appointment.

This select group of people has already heard of your store and knows what you have in stock. For example, now that the college grad knows she wants to lease a Ruby Red Metallic Ford Escape SE with an EcoBoost engine, you have an opportunity to show her the next step. And now that the family of four is ready for a test drive, your store can be their first (and possibly only) stop.

Since you've already tailored and delivered a helpful message and qualified your audience, you have an opportunity to guide them across the finish line.

ANSWER THE RIGHT QUESTIONS

MESSENGER FORMAT   **MOBILE PLACEMENT**   **RUN UP TO 3 MONTHS**   **SETUP DIFFICULTY**

RECOMMENDED AUDIENCES

- A retargeting audience of people with several VDP/SRP views within the last 15 days

- A custom audience of unsold leads who converted within the last 15 days

At the bottom of the funnel, you know who your leads are. These potential customers have looked at specific products on your website and are in the consideration stage.

A Messenger ad lets you humanize your business online. By showing this type of ad to qualified leads, you can suggest trade evaluations or test drives, encourage real questions, and give a timely, helpful answer.

The key here is to have someone at your dealership who will respond quickly. Include a friendly photo of this person on your Messenger ad. Once they've initiated the conversation and identified the lead's needs, they can then pass the contact and their information along to your sales team.

JADEN MILLER

Major World Chrysler Jeep Dodge Ram

Sponsored ·

The only way to truly know if a vehicle is right for you is to drive it for yourself!

We make it easy to test drive the vehicle that catches your eye. Complete a few short steps and we'll get your drive time scheduled!

Schedule Your Test Drive | **View Nev Jeep, and**

1 Share

 Like   Comment   Share

GET THEIR HANDS ON THE WHEEL

CAROUSEL FORMAT   **MOBILE & DESKTOP**   **RUN UP TO 1 MONTH**   **SETUP DIFFICULTY**

RECOMMENDED AUDIENCES

- People who are actively shopping for certain models

- Third-party targeting for in-market shoppers of certain models

- A custom audience of unsold leads interested in certain models who have not interacted with emails or phone calls

It can be frustrating to watch your list of unsold leads grow from month to month. That's why we came up with this recipe to make the pathway to purchase more clear for even your most stubborn contacts.

This carousel takes the ever-churning list of qualified leads to the bottom of the funnel for Major World CDJR, where people can choose to either set an appointment or continue researching inventory.

A well-designed scheduling page is ideal for the first card in this ad, but you could also send people to a contact page where they can request an appointment with a form submission.

JACQUELYN JACOBSMA

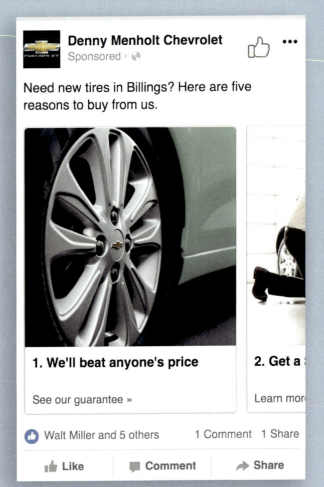

CONVINCE WITH CUSTOMER SERVICE

CAROUSEL FORMAT   **MOBILE PLACEMENT**   **RUN UP TO 1 MONTH**   **SETUP DIFFICULTY** 5/10

RECOMMENDED AUDIENCES

- A retargeting audience of people who have viewed VDPs or SRPs

- A custom audience of current leads who last purchased vehicles more than four years ago

- Unsold qualified leads who have not engaged with emails or phone calls

Help bottom-of-funnel leads by putting yourself out there as their number-one place to buy. How do service ads help sales? There are countless ways to sell vehicles using bottom-of-funnel Facebook ads, but service is also a good way to illustrate your commitment to customers.

A Montana Chevy dealer sought to promote tire sales and check in with qualified leads who had purchased a vehicle more than four years ago and who had also expressed interest in auto service.

Bottom-of-funnel ads are all about converting leads, so keep conversion top of mind when measuring the success of these ads.

SARAH KLONGERBO

STAY WITH YOUR QUALIFIED LEADS

| CAROUSEL FORMAT | MOBILE PLACEMENT | RUN UP TO 1 MONTH | SETUP DIFFICULTY |

RECOMMENDED AUDIENCES

- People who have browsed new vehicle VDPs in the last 15-30 days

INTEGRATIONS

- Facebook pixel
- Cumulus (by 9 Clouds)

We've already covered dynamic retargeting recipes in the top and middle sections of the funnel, but this impressive technology can also carry your leads through the sale.

The Cumulus software by 9 Clouds connects Chastang CDJR's inventory feed to VIN-specific retargeting carousel ads. At the bottom of the funnel, this connection allows Chastang to run continously at the bottom of their strategy, in conjunction with the store's other time-bound campaigns at the top and middle of the funnel.

Set a daily budget for these campaigns, and you'll create a steady flow of qualified traffic — and a measurable lift in Offline Events.

ALLEN DAY

EVALUATE THE TRADE

| LEAD AD FORMAT | MOBILE PLACEMENT | RUN UP TO 1 MONTH | SETUP DIFFICULTY |

RECOMMENDED AUDIENCES

- Current customers who have owned their vehicles for more than two years

- People who own sought-after vehicles that meet certain criteria

The bottom of the funnel is where we convert qualified contacts into leads. Facebook's lead ad format pre-fills with known values, such as name, email, and phone number. Plus, you can add your own questions to gather relevant data.

This ad recipe is especially useful for dealers that do not currently have landing pages specifically for collecting information for trade evaluations.

For this ad, we first created the trade evaluation form within Facebook Business Manager with the fields the dealership wanted. We then used a service called LeadsBridge to connect the lead/eval data directly into the dealer's CRM.

 JOHN NELSON

OPTIMIZING ADS FOR YOUR DEALERSHIP

FACEBOOK SPLIT/CONTENT TESTING

With any kind of advertising, there's a temptation to go with your gut. That's a great way to come up with new ideas to try. But when you get down to trying to determine which targeting and ads work best for you on Facebook, it's a good idea to do a little content testing.

Mimicking the scientific method, you want to run two ads or ad sets against each other with as few differences as possible (ideally just one variable).

For ad sets, you can do this pretty easily by cloning an ad set within the same campaign and making one change to the copy. Let them both run, and see which does better at the end of a set time period.

For ads, the process is similar. Just clone the ad for which you want to try something different within the same ad set, and see which prevails. You can judge success by clicks, CTR, or — if you've been tagging your ads — data from Google Analytics.

Facebook is going to prioritize the better-performing ad within an ad set, so if your ad sets share a budget in a campaign, one can get out ahead of the other. But this is a simple way to settle the debate on which picture or CTA button works best for an ad, or whether you get better results targeting in-market shoppers or your website visitors.

Now, Facebook is working on a split-testing tool that will let you do this all a bit more accurately, dividing audiences 50/50. There are some kinks it's still working out, but you can keep an eye on updates at 9clouds.com/blog.

Content testing lets you improve your Facebook ad game. Without spending the full time and money of a campaign, you're learning which tactics work best with measurable data points.

Happy testing!

GUARANTEE YOUR SUCCESS

Facebook advertising is here to stay. In fact, its power is only growing as we spend more time on our phones and social networks.

Increasingly, the future of advertising looks like a digital duopoly of Google (the "what") and Facebook (the "who"). As Scott Galloway notes in *The Four*:

> Google and Facebook are redrawing the media map. Eventually they will control more media spend than any two firms in history — separately, much less combined. Facebook and Google control 51 percent of global mobile ad spend, and their share grows every day. In 2016, the two firms accounted for 103% of all digital media revenue growth.[4]

This means that, sans Facebook and Google, digital media now joins

newspapers, radio, and broadcast TV as sectors that are in decline.[5] For auto dealers — and businesses everywhere — now is the time to start with Facebook advertising. Any competitor can log in to Facebook and access the same potential buyers, so long-term success requires a custom approach that gathers and uses data to attract customers.

Dealers that begin tracking their website visitors, connecting their inventory, and targeting past customers and leads from their CRM enjoy an advantage. They can target specific people who may be unavailable to other dealers.

The future of digital advertising is right in front of us. Learn to use Facebook now to guarantee your current and future success.

TAKE ACTION
9 CLOUDS CAN HELP

This book is one way to get started with professional Facebook advertising. Our digital marketing company, 9 Clouds, can help you take the next step whether you are looking to do it yourself, do it with some help, or hire someone else to help you.

Visit *9clouds.com/facebook* to learn more about any of these options, read our latest blog posts, or watch our training videos.

DO IT MYSELF

Improve conversion from your Facebook advertising with Cumulus.

Cumulus connects automotive inventory feeds with your Facebook catalog, so you can show cars to people likely to buy cars. It's perfect for advanced marketers and agencies.

The best part? These ads are fully dynamic, meaning that the image, text, and price of vehicles shown all change automatically based on your current inventory feed.

If you sell a vehicle, that vehicle is automatically removed from your ad. If you acquire a new vehicle, it is automatically added to your ads.

We have seen three times higher CTR and engagement with these ads — all with little management required after launch.

DO IT TOGETHER

Learn the best practices of Facebook marketing through our education and consulting.

Our courses help you create automotive ads that convert on Facebook. They include worksheets and video training, so it is easy for you to take what you learn and immediately apply it to your store or clients.

9 Clouds also works with a small number of consulting clients on a monthly basis. These trainings are available both virtually (through screen-sharing and weekly calls) or as in-person training sessions.

DO IT FOR ME

Work with our team of experts for Facebook ads customized for your store.

9 Clouds offers full-service digital marketing focused on search engine optimization (SEO), online ads on Facebook and Google, email marketing, and lead tracking. We often work as the digital quarterback, coordinating your vendors so your digital marketing is focused, measured, and complementary.

We also offer Facebook advertising services on an à la carte basis.

Our team will create and measure all your campaigns in your Facebook Business Manager, so you have full access to everything we do. Plus, we take 0% of your monthly ad spend budget, so we can objectively help you find the most effective budget for your market.

We are constantly testing and learning what works best online. We take these lessons from stores around the United States and Canada to create custom, personalized campaigns for your store. Every account comes with the personal service you would expect from a boutique agency based in Sioux Falls, South Dakota.

ONE LAST NOTE:

If you enjoyed this book, please rate it on Amazon and share it with your fellow automotive marketing friends.

Order more copies and find more resources at:

9clouds.com/facebook/fieldguide

Thank You

Made in the USA
Lexington, KY
27 June 2018

Thank You

Made in the USA
Lexington, KY
27 June 2018